Rainforest Birds

Elizabeth Nonweiler

antshrike

bee-eaters

puffbird

pied hornbill

common potoo

scarlet macaw

white cockatoo

plush-crested jay

snail kite

river kingfisher

blue-chested
hummingbird

lesser bird
of paradise

13

Interesting facts about the pictures

page 2: **Antshrikes** live in the Amazon rainforest and sometimes follow swarms of ants. They have a notch at the top of their bills to help them hold and crush insects before they eat them.

page 3: The **bee-eaters** that live in the rainforest in Africa are called blue-headed bee-eaters. They perch in high branches and then swoop down to catch butterflies, bees or other insects.

page 4: **Puffbirds** live in South America and Mexico. They have lots of loose feathers that make them look stout and puffy. They lay their eggs in holes in the ground lined with dry leaves.

page 5: This is a great **pied hornbill** from Asia. It has a wingspan of about 1.5 metres and can live for nearly 50 years. When it looks for a mate, the male calls "kok" and a female calls back.

page 6: This **common potoo** sleeps with its chick. At night its eyes reflect the light, but in the day it stays still on a branch that is the same colour as its feathers. Then it is almost invisible.

page 7: **Scarlet macaws** live in South America. They eat fruits, nuts and seeds. They lay two or three white eggs in a hole in a tree and the chicks stay with their parents for about a year.

page 8: **White cockatoos** live in Indonesia. Sometimes people keep them as pets, because they are friendly, clever and beautiful. If they are kept in a cage, though, they cannot fly when they want to.

page 9: **Plush-crested jays** are found in South America. They make more than 20 different sounds: loud to defend territory, low for family and friends, and "chyup-chyip" when they find food.

page 10: **Snail kites** live in South America, Florida and the Caribbean. They fly slowly, looking for snails to eat. They nest in bushes or on the ground, laying three or four eggs.

page 11: **River kingfishers** are found in Australia, Asia, Africa and Europe. They dig burrows to lay their eggs in and both parents feed the chicks. This one has just caught a fish.

page 12: **Blue-chested hummingbirds** are found in Central America. They are very small – less than 14 centimetres long. When they fly, they flap their wings so fast they make a humming sound.

page 13: The **lesser bird of paradise** lives in New Guinea. The male bird dances and shows off his beautiful feathers to impress the female. Then the female builds a nest for their eggs.

Letter-sound correspondences

Level 2 books cover the following letter-sound correspondences.
Letter-sound correspondences highlighted in green can be found in this book.

ant	big	cat	dog	egg	fish	get	hot	it
jet	key	let	man	nut	off	pan	queen	run
sun	tap	up	van	wet	box	yes	zoo	
duck	fish	chips	sing	thin this	keep	look moon	art	corn

say	boy	rain	oil	boat	eat	pie	high
make	these	like	note	flute tube	out	saw	author
her	bird	turn	airport	flew stew	blue cue	phone	when

16